LEVEL 2 SCIENCE

LET'S READ AND FIND OUT

WHAT WILL THE WEATHER BE?

BY LYNDA DEWITT

ILLUSTRATED BY CAROLYN CROLL

HARPER

An Imprint of HarperCollinsPublishers

Special thanks to Dr. Sean Birkel of the Climate Change Institute at the University of Maine for his expert advice.

The Let's-Read-and-Find-Out Science book series was originated by Dr. Franklyn M. Branley, Astronomer Emeritus and former Chairman of the American Museum of Natural History–Hayden Planetarium, and was formerly co-edited by him and Dr. Roma Gans, Professor Emeritus of Childhood Education, Teachers College, Columbia University. Text and illustrations for each of the books in the series are checked for accuracy by an expert in the relevant field. For more information about Let's-Read-and-Find-Out Science books, write to HarperCollins Children's Books, 195 Broadway, New York, NY 10007, or visit our website at www.letsreadandfindout.com.

Let's Read-and-Find-Out Science® is a trademark of HarperCollins Publishers.

Library of Congress Cataloging-in-Publication Data
DeWitt, Lynda.
   What will the weather be? / by Lynda DeWitt ; illustrated by Carolyn Croll.
      p.   cm. — (Let's-read-and-find-out science. Stage 2)
   Summary: Explains the basic characteristics of weather—temperature, humidity, wind speed and direction, air pressure—and how meteorologists gather data for their forecasts.
   ISBN 978-0-06-238198-9
   1. Weather forecasting—Juvenile literature.   [1. Weather forecasting.]   I. Croll, Carolyn, ill.   II. Title.   III. Series.
QC995.43.D48   1991   90-1446
551.6'3—dc20   CIP
                                                                                                                              AC

15   16   17   18   19   SCP   10   9   8   7   6   5   4   3   2   1

❖

Revised edition, 2015

WHAT WILL THE WEATHER BE?

4

The sky was gray and cloudy over Washington, D.C., on the morning of March 9, 1999. The weather forecast called for an inch or two of snow.

5

But by noon, there was so much snow on the ground that many cars and buses were stuck in it. The airports had to close down. So did the schools. In all, eight inches of snow fell on the city.

The weather forecast was wrong. And people were not prepared for the huge storm.

Weather forecasts tell us what kind of weather is coming.
But predicting the weather is hard to do.
It is easy to see what the weather is like right now.
You can go outside and look. Is the air warm or cold?
Is it windy or still? Is the sky clear?
Or is it covered with dark clouds?

Whatever the weather is like, it often stays that way
for days at a time.

But then something happens.
The wind begins to blow. Air from somewhere else moves in.

FRONT

Old Air

Sometimes it is cooler air from the north.
Sometimes it is warmer air from the south.
The new air pushes against the old air.
The place where this happens is called a front.
Most changes in the weather occur along fronts.

Where cold air pushes against warm air, we say
there is a cold front.

Cold fronts move fast. They can make the wind howl.
They quickly push warm air up and out of the way.
The rising air carries water. The water is not a liquid.
It is a gas called water vapor.

As the air rises, it cools, and the water vapor turns to liquid.
High in the sky, the drops of liquid water clump together
and make clouds.

cold air

COLD FRONT

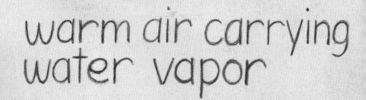

warm air carrying
water vapor

The clouds grow big and dark as more air rises.
Then it rains. There may be thunder and lightning.

If it is cold enough, snow falls. It all happens very fast.
Cold fronts cause sudden storms, but they usually
do not last long. After a cold front passes, the sky clears
and the weather is colder.

Where warm air pushes against cold air, a warm front forms.
Warm fronts move slowly. They make the wind blow just a little.
Wispy clouds cover the sky.

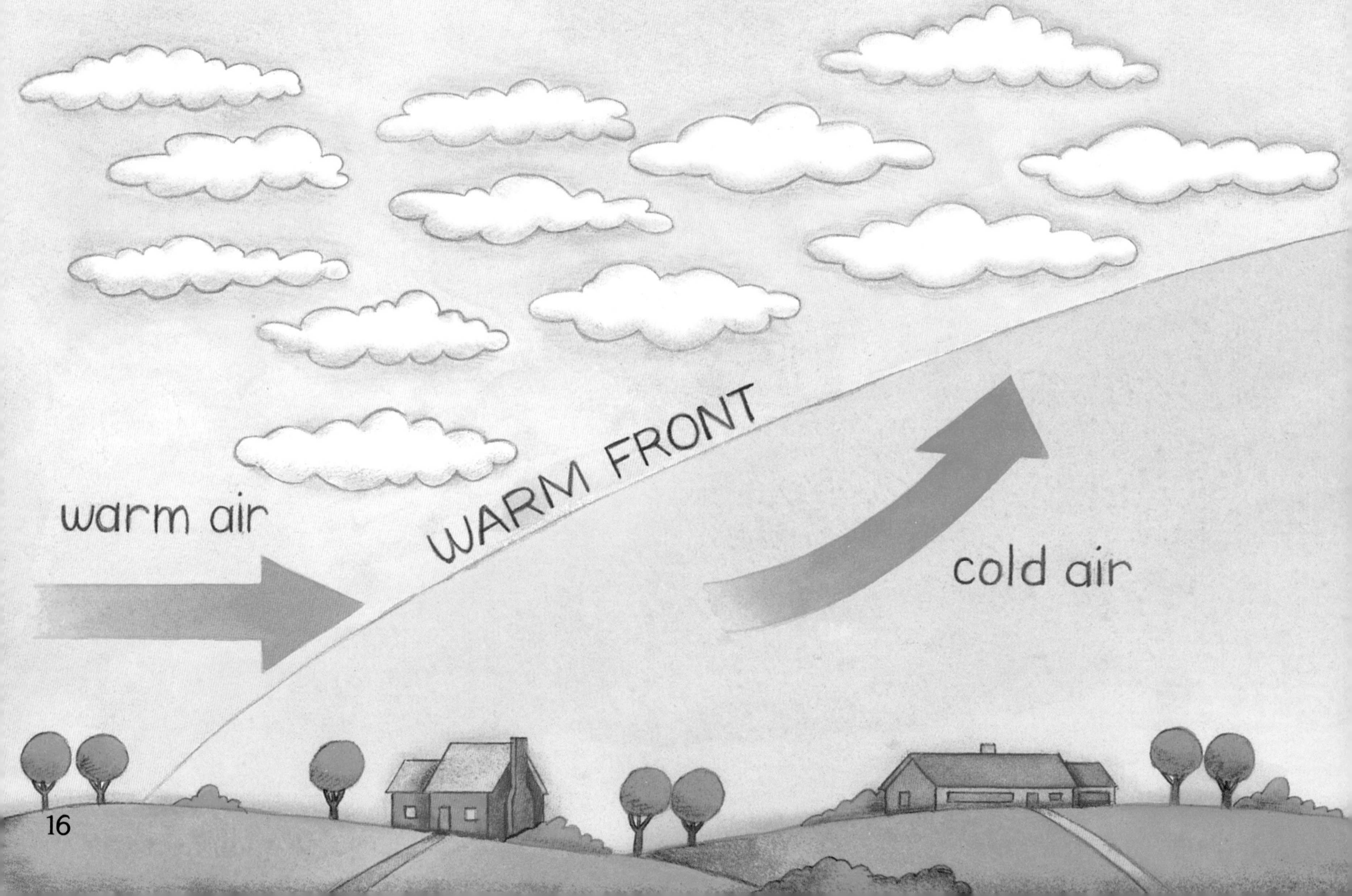

warm air

WARM FRONT

cold air

There may be a light shower. Or it may drizzle for a couple of days.

Warm fronts change the weather slowly. After a warm front passes, the sky clears and the weather is warmer.

Meteorologists, people who study the weather, try to predict where fronts will form.

They measure the temperature of the air at different places around the earth. They find out where the warm air is and where the cold air is.

A wind vane tells from what direction the wind blows.

wind vane

They watch to see where the air moves.
They measure how fast it goes.

An anemometer measures wind speed.

anemometer

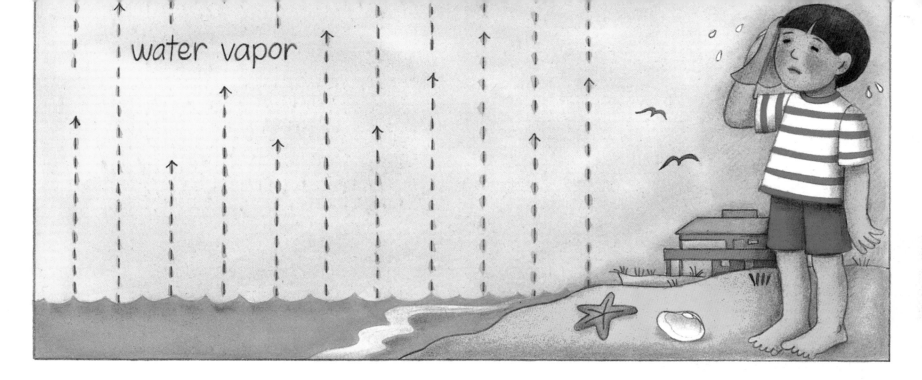

water vapor

Meteorologists also measure the amount of water vapor, or humidity, in the air.

Water vapor is what makes air feel damp, or humid. Lots of water vapor rises from the ocean. That is why air along coastlines feels humid.

A hygrometer measures humidity.

hygrometer

21

Another thing meteorologists measure is air pressure. It's hard to imagine, but air has weight. And all of this weight presses on the earth. It presses on everything—even you! Hundreds of pounds of air press against your body all the time. You cannot feel it because air inside your body pushes out with the same force.

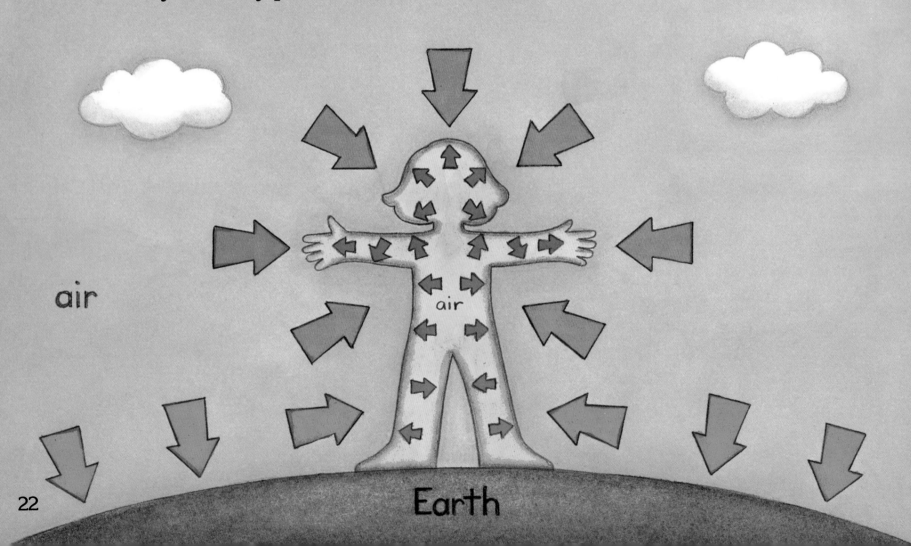

air

air

Earth

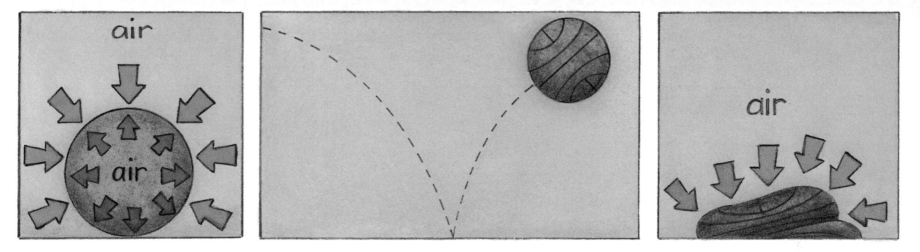

Air inside this basketball pushes out, too. You can bounce a ball when it has air in it. But what happens when you take the air out? The basketball flattens. It collapses from the weight of outside air.

You cannot feel air pressure, and you cannot tell when it changes. But it does. Sometimes it is high, and sometimes it is low. As the air pressure changes, the weather changes.

A barometer measures air pressure.

When air pressure is low, air is rising into the sky.
Water vapor in the air turns to liquid and clouds form.
As more air rises, the pressure gets lower and lower.
And the clouds get bigger and darker.
Lots of rain or snow may fall when the air pressure is low.

When air pressure is high, air is sinking toward earth.
The skies stay mostly clear.
A few puffy clouds may appear, but it won't rain.
The weather is dry and sunny when the air pressure is high.

Meteorologists measure the air pressure over the whole earth.
They find the highs and the lows.
They measure the temperature and humidity of the air.
They see where air is warm or cold, damp or dry.
They measure the speed and direction of the wind.
They take their measurements over the oceans and over the land.

weather buoy

weather satellite

weather airplane

weather balloon

weather station

27

Throughout the day the measurements are sent to the National Weather Service in Maryland. There, huge computers plot the measurements on maps. The maps show the temperature, humidity, and pressure of the air all around the world. Arrows on the maps mark the direction of the winds. Cold fronts and warm fronts show where storms are forming.

Meteorologists everywhere study the maps. To forecast weather for tomorrow and the next day, they need to know what is happening hundreds and hundreds of miles away. They need to know what kind of air is coming. Then they can make their forecasts.

Weather Map

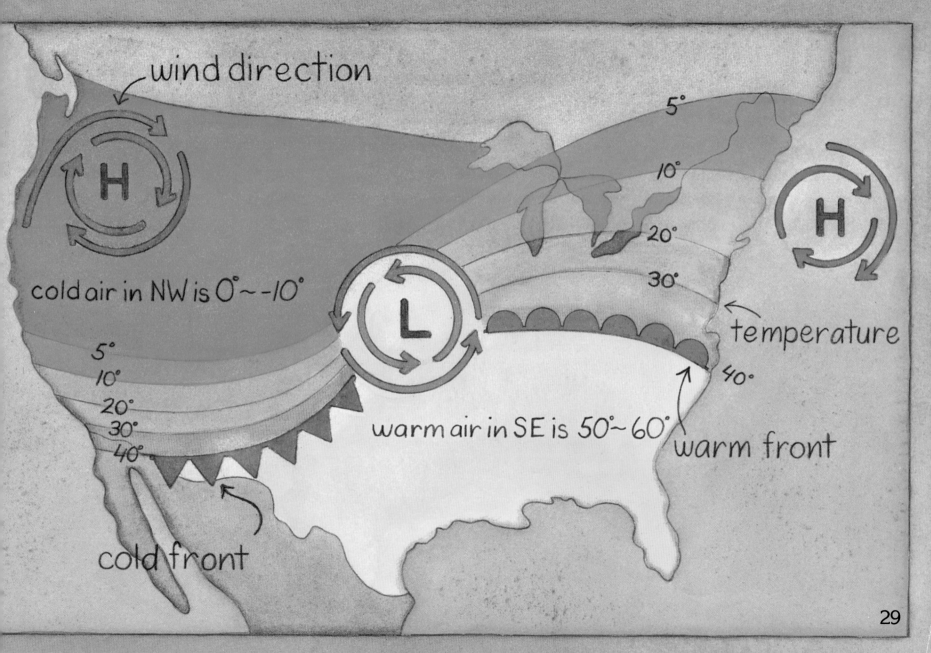

Weather forecasts are broadcast over radio and television stations, and can also be found online or in the newspapers. The forecasts tell us what kind of air is coming and what kind of weather to expect.

They may call for warm and sunny days.

Or they may tell us to prepare for snow and strong winds.

They warn farmers when a frost is coming.

They help us decide whether our schools and airports should be closed down.

Changes in the weather are not always predictable.
So not all of the forecasts are right.
Sometimes meteorologists tell us to take our umbrellas
when we don't need them. Other times they say we
won't need a jacket when we do.

But meteorologists today know more about the
weather than ever before. And usually we can depend
on their forecasts when we're wondering,
"What will the weather be?"

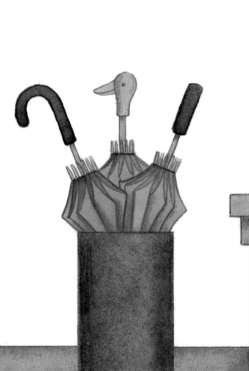